HEATHCLIFF FIRST PRIZE!

The funniest feline in America delights millions of fans every day as he appears in over 500 newspapers. You'll have a laugh a minute as Heathcliff tangles with the milkman, the fish store owner, the tuna fisherman and just about everyone else he runs into. If you're looking for some fun, look no further, Heathcliff is here.

HEATHCLIFF®
FIRST PRIZE!

by

Geo Gately

C

CHARTER BOOKS, NEW YORK

HEATHCLIFF FIRST PRIZE!

A Charter Book / published by arrangement with
Licensed Ventures International, Ltd.

PRINTING HISTORY
Charter Original / September 1984

Charter Books are published by The Berkley Publishing Group,
200 Madison Avenue, New York, New York 10016.
PRINTED IN THE UNITED STATES OF AMERICA

"THIS DEPARTMENT IS RIDDLED
WITH DISSENSION!"

"I FIXED THAT CUPBOARD
SO IT DOESN'T STICK."

"PLAY IT AGAIN, SAM!"

"...AND HOW ABOUT HEATHCLIFF?...DOES HE
HAVE A HALLOWEEN COSTUME?"

"NO THANKS... I'VE ALREADY SEEN
THIS MORNING'S PAPER."

"HI, COACH!...HOW'D THE TEAM PICTURE TURN OUT?"

"IT'S SO HARD TO WEAN THEM OFF GANG RUMBLES!"

"JUST SMELL THIS, HARRY!....
CATS WILL GO MAD FOR IT!"

" HE'S OVER THERE... WORKING OUT ON THE HEAVY BAG. "

"WHAT'D HE PULL IN CANADA ?!"

"AW...HE'S SO CUTE, I JUST CAN'T BRING MYSELF TO TAKE HIM IN."

"HMMM...HE DOES HAVE BEADY LITTLE EYES!"

"SNEAK BY HEATHCLIFF, BUT YOU WON'T SNEAK BY ME!"

"WE'VE GOT HIM TRAPPED!...GO UP THERE
AND GET HIM!!"

"WHY DON'T YOU GIVE HIM A TRANQUILIZER?"

"I DID."

"HE'S TRYING TO FADE HIS DESIGNER JEANS."

"YOU DON'T LIKE OUR ALL NEW
NON-DAIRY CREAMER?"

"HOW LONG BEFORE THE RIBBON CUTTING CEREMONY TAKES PLACE ?!"

"SOME OF THESE CHARITIES ARE DOWNRIGHT PUSHY!"

"THERE'S NO WAY OF GETTING HIS ATTENTION DURING FOOTBALL SEASON!"

"IF YOU'D STOP BELTING THEM AROUND, YOU WOULDN'T HAVE TO BRING THEM HERE!"

"WATCH OUT FOR YOUR FOOT!"

"HE DROPPED A LARGE BULLDOG ON IT."

"FIFTEEN YARD PENALTY...ILLEGAL USE
OF SCRATCHING POST!"

"THE NUTMEG RESIDENCE?... DOWN THIS ROAD
ABOUT A HALF MI.....

....JUST FOLLOW THE CEMENT!"

"I DON'T HAVE ANY OLD ARMY BUDDIES...
I WAS IN THE COASTGUARD."

"HAH!...YOU MISSED THE SPARE!"

"THEY HAD MICE IN THEIR FILE CABINET."

"THAT'S A VERY EFFECTIVE FLEA COLLAR!"

"COMING UP!...AFTER THESE MESSAGES!...
GARBAGE DUMPING AS AN ART FORM!"

"THERE GOES
CRAZY SHIRLEY!...

...SHE FAINTS AT ALL
OF HIS CONCERTS."

1981
McNaught Synd., Inc.

"TODAY, CLASS, I THINK WE'LL CANCEL
'SHOW AND TELL'."

"IT'S THE BULLDOG EDITION."

"VOLLEYBALL !!"

"MY GOSH!...YOU'D THINK A PARADE
MARCHED THROUGH HERE!"

" COMFY?!! "

"GET AWAY!...YOU BOTHER
THE MONKEY!"

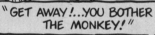

" TOO BAD WE COULDN'T BRING HEATHCLIFF. "

"HI, MR. TURTLE!"

"HE'S TRYING TO BRING BACK THE BIG BANDS!"

"CRAZY SHIRLEY!!"

".... MUST BE A 'SINGLES' BAR."

" I THINK SHE'D PREFER AN APPLE. "

"THE QUARTERBACK FADES..."

"...FAKES A HANDOFF TO BRONKURSKI..."

"...AND HITS SWIFTY WITH A LONG ONE."

".....I'LL DIAGRAM THE PLAYS!"

"DID WE SWALLOW
OUR VITAMINS?"

" EVER BUY ONE ?! "

" I FIND YOU....

....IN CONTEMPT OF COURT. "

"VAMOOSE, PODNUH!"

"I'M GOING TO PRACTICE NOW."

"WILL YOU STOP WITH THOSE CHIPMUNKS?!"

"MAYBE I SHOULD JUST GO TO THE DENTIST!"

"AH! IT'S NICE TO SEE THAT CHIVALRY ISN'T DEAD!"

"NO...BUT YOUR PLAID SHIRT IS!"

"SOUNDS LIKE A LITTLE INDIGESTION."

10-30
© 1981
McNaught Synd., Inc.

"WHY, IT'S CRAZY SHIRLEY!...I NEVER
WOULD HAVE GUESSED!"

"WE WON'T HARM THE TUNA!"

"I'M IMPRESSED WITH YOUR NEW WATCHDOG!"

"IF YOU DON'T LIKE IT, JUST SEND US
A NASTY LETTER!"

"THEY'RE INTO MUD WRESTLING!"

"THESE GUYS CLAIM THEY PAID FOR BOX SEATS!"

"SORRY TO KEEP YOU WAITING SO LONG."

"YOU ARRANGED THIS, DIDN'T YOU?!"

"GO GET 'IM, DANDY!"

"ATTA BOY, DANDY! YEA, DANDY!"

"C'MON, RAGS."

"...EIGHTY-FIVE CENTS...A PETE ROSE BUBBLE GUM CARD...
A LAWRENCE WELK ALBUM...CRAZY SHIRLEY'S DOWRY."

"I'M NOT AMUSED."

"IS THAT YOUR NOSE OR
ARE YOU EATING AN APPLE?"

"NO SENSE OF HUMOR!"

"YOU BETTER QUIT PLAYING THESE MACHINES ALL DAY!"

"HE'S SO TERRIBLY BUSY, HE CAN'T TAKE TIME
TO EAT AT HOME !"

"NO, THIS ISN'T THE LUMBER YARD."

"YOU'VE GOT HARRY'S 'BEEF AND BREW'
OR HEATHCLIFF'S 'DUMP AND DINE'."

"HAH! I'LL NAB YOU WITH THE GOODS THIS TIME!"

"THIS IS HIS BOWLING NIGHT."

"HE'S NARROWED IT DOWN TO A BURT REYNOLDS
OR A CLINT EASTWOOD."

"HE'S EXPANDING HIS TERRITORY AGAIN!"

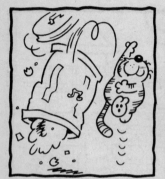

"SORRY, NO SUBSTITUTIONS."

"WE'RE TRYING TO AVOID A CERTAIN CAT."

"HE LOVES THIS PLACE!"

"SO MUCH FOR YOUR SPITE FENCE!"

"THE SEWER COVER IS HOME AND THIS GUY IS FIRST BASE."

"YOU GAVE ME AN
AWFUL FRIGHT!"

"I'M SURE WE'RE ALL IMPRESSED WITH THE STORY
OF HIS TRAGIC CHILDHOOD, COUNSELOR!"

"HE CAN'T DECIDE BETWEEN 'ALOOF' AND 'MACHO'."

"....SO GOOD YOUR CAT WILL DEMAND MORE!"

"THIS IS CALLED 'RODENT IN REPOSE'."

"HI...I'M THE CAT SITTER."

" DON'T CALL HIM TO SUPPER WHEN I'M ....

....FOLDING LAUNDRY."

"HE ENJOYS DINNER AND THEATRE OCCASIONALLY."

"HE'S TEACHING HIS SON THE BUSINESS!"

"WHEN I'M NOT CHASING DOGS FOR THE CITY POUND,
MY PERSONAL LIFE IS NO CONCERN OF YOURS!"

"ATTACKED BY A GIANT SQUID?!"

"DINNER FOR TWO?"

"WHAT'S YOUR SIGN DOING NEXT DOOR?"

"GO OVER THERE AND GET IT."

"HIJACKING IS A SERIOUS OFFENSE!"

"WE SHOULD HAVE GONE
TO THE MOUNTAINS...

...INSTEAD OF
THE SHORE."

"ADMITTEDLY, SIX CENTS ISN'T VERY MUCH."

"I'M GLAD YOU STOWED AWAY WITH YOUR
SCRATCHING POST!"

"HE'LL NEVER FORGIVE THEM FOR THE BASEBALL STRIKE!"

"YOU CALLED IT!"

"THE OCEAN'S ROAR WAS BROUGHT TO YOU TODAY BY 'WHOOPEE CAT FOOD'."

"IT DOESN'T COME IN THAT SIZE."

"YOU DON'T HAVE TO BRING US THE EVIDENCE!"

" HAVE YOU GOT A CLAMMING LICENSE ? "

"TAKE YOUR SCRATCHING POST AND GO HOME!"

"YOU'VE BEEN SPRUNG.... SEE THAT
YOU KEEP YOUR NOSE CLEAN!"

"BE NICE.... SHE'S BUILDING A NEST."

"SO YUMMY!...SO SOFT!...SO CHEWABLE!..."

"I'D SWEAR I HEARD A TWIG SNAP!"

"YOU'RE BLOCKING HIS TAN."

"MARVELOUS!...THE MISSING SHINBONE
OF THE STEGOSAURUS!"

"ARE THEY TELLING SPOOKY STORIES AGAIN?"

"NO NEED TO BRING YOUR OWN TEABAG!"

"EEK!!"

"HOW SWEET!... HIS MOTHER'S BROOCH!"

"THAT REMINDS ME!... I MUST INVITE
MY MOTHER OVER FOR A VISIT!"

"IT'S BROAD IN THE BEAM AND HARD TO HANDLE!"

© 1981
McNaught Synd., Inc.

"HE'S WITH THE TUNA LOBBY!"

"CLOSE THAT PARASOL AND YOU'LL FIT!"

"HE WANTS US TO RAISE THE DRAWBRIDGE!"

"YOUR DESIGNER JEANS ARE TOO TIGHT."

"I'LL DO THE EXAMINING!"

"HELP!"

"JUST USE IT AS A SCRATCHING POST!"

"HOW'S BUSINESS?"

"KNOCK OFF THE SING-ALONG!"